I0460607

Rare on Purpose
© 2025 Jay Floyd

First Edition

Cover design by Jay Floyd
Interior design by Jay Floyd

Published by Jay Floyd Books
www.iamjayfloyd.com

Printed in the United States of America

This book is a work of nonfiction. All personal stories and experiences are true to the author's knowledge. In cases where names or identifying details have been changed, it is to respect privacy.

Introduction

Read This Before You Go Looking for Yourself

You don't need a new version of you. You need a better memory.

Because you've been rare the whole time. But life has a way of making you forget.

And when you forget your shape, it doesn't just cost you opportunity—it can cost you joy, peace, your voice, even whole seasons you don't get back.

You start out believing you were made for something. You feel it. In your gut. In your bones. But life starts loading you down.

You shrink parts of yourself so other people stay comfortable. You play it safe, because risk feels reckless when you've got bills to pay. You trade passion for predictability. You start doing what you're good at instead of what you're here for. You get praised for being reliable and forget what it feels like to be powerful.

And little by little, the rare part of you gets buried.

You look up one day and think: "Is this it?"

If that's you—let's be real:

You are not average. You are not easy to replace. You are not "just" a parent, or a manager, or a creative who can't seem to land. You are not just a survivor of hard things.

You are you. And that is the most powerful thing you can bring into any room, any relationship, any role.

But when you've spent years shrinking, performing, adapting—it's hard to remember your real shape.

So let's cut through the noise.

This book? It's here to help you remember.

It's not a manual. It's not here to hype you up for a week.

It's a mirror. A flashlight. A scalpel—if you're ready to cut through some lies.

We're not chasing trends. We're returning to design.

Because in a world obsessed with automation, the most powerful, unforgettable thing you can be is fully human. Not a product of pressure—but a person shaped by it. Not the sum of your job titles—but the shape life forged in you when no one was watching.

More people than you think are walking around feeling like imposters in their own lives. They're not broken. They're just misaligned.

So if you've ever: – Felt boxed in by your role – Wondered if your voice still matters – Or doubted whether there's still something rare in you worth activating...

You're not too late. You're just overdue.

I know what it's like to stay too long in a role that no longer fits. To ignore the edge God gave you just to keep the peace. To convince yourself that safety is more important than alignment.

But I also know what happens when you stop performing and start becoming.

That's why we're here.

To remember what got buried. To name what makes you rare. To build a life that matches your shape.

And by the end of this book, you won't just remember who you are— You'll know exactly how to move like it.

Let's be rare. On purpose. You take a job just to survive. Shrink parts of yourself so other people stay comfortable. Play it safe, because risk feels reckless when you've got bills to pay. Trade passion for predictability. You start doing what you're good at instead of what you're here for. Get praised for being reliable and forget what it feels like to be powerful.

You're not just invited into this work. You're responsible for it now.

Phase I: Remember Your Rare

This isn't about becoming someone else. It's about waking up to who you've always been.

You don't have to chase purpose like it's missing. You just have to stop forgetting where it lives.

This phase is about that remembering.

Before we talk about goals or titles— we're going back to the root. Back to the voice you muted. Back to the strengths you learned to downplay. And to the fire you thought you had to hide.

We're digging under the résumé, the expectations, and the mask.

We're unearthing your shape. The fire you tucked away. The wiring God already gave you. The parts of you that weren't broken—they were buried.

By the end of this phase, you won't have it all figured out. But you'll know what's been in you the whole time.

Let's remember it. Let's reclaim it. Let's move like it's always mattered. But you'll have language. And language leads to movement.

Chapter 1: You've Been Rare the Whole Time

Rediscovering your identity through lived experience, not hype.

You don't need a new title. You need to remember your name.

Before we talk careers or strengths, let's start somewhere more personal.

Let's talk about who you've always been.

Let's talk about your name.

Because a name isn't just what shows up in your inbox. It's a signal. A story. A shape. Sometimes it carries legacy before you even know how to wear it.

That name on the cover? That's not just branding. That's me saying: I'm not offering a product. I'm offering perspective.

This isn't a lecture. It's a conversation. Between two people tired of shrinking to fit.

I'm not writing at you. I'm writing to you.

My name is Jay Floyd. That's the one you'll see in the podcast feed or the email signature. But my full name is Jason Edward Floyd.

And that middle name? That's where the story starts.

My mom grew up in a small Mississippi town where names carried weight.

She had a younger brother—my uncle—named Edward. But nobody called him that. To my grandmother, he was her Jewel. Her favorite. Her heart.

When they moved north, her Mississippi accent came with her. And when she said "Jewel," people misheard it as "Gerald." Then assumed it started with a J. So they started calling him Jay.

Edward became Jay—by accident, by accent, by love.

And when I was born, my mom didn't give me his name directly. She gave me Jason Edward.

But I chose to go by Jay.

Not because I needed a nickname— but because I wanted to live up to what I saw in him.

Jay wasn't just a name. It was a presence.

Uncle Jay didn't need to be loud to be legendary. He had that quiet gravity—the kind that makes rooms adjust.

He didn't chase attention. He just showed up fully. And that was more than enough.

He moved like someone who knew exactly who he was. And somehow, even in silence, everybody else knew it too.

Cool without trying. Sharp without performing. He became the moment without saying a word.

He looked at you like you mattered. And you started believing maybe you did.

I didn't inherit his full name. But I inherited his shape.

And even before I saw that shape in myself— It was already in me.

I didn't earn Jay. But I've spent my life learning how to wear it.

Because even what's gifted must be guarded. Even what's inherited must be practiced.

We forget that sometimes.

We think rare must be invented. Packaged. Marketed. Monetized.

But sometimes, rare isn't something you create. It's something you stop editing.

Rare shows up in how you carry what others avoid. In the way you rebound after being overlooked. In how you lead with presence when others perform.

Rare doesn't always roar. Sometimes it whispers.

But it's real.

It shows up in your wiring— The way your gut knows before your brain does. The way your heart holds space for people who never held space for you. The way your "too much" becomes a tool—once you stop apologizing for it.

That rare didn't just arrive one day. It's been buried under expectations. Flattened by image. Dismissed by systems that couldn't quantify it.

Whispering beneath the noise: "You still in there?"

You've been rare the whole time. Not because of what you've done. But because of what was planted in you.

Rare isn't earned. It's revealed.

And this book? It's a mirror. A flashlight. A manual for remembering what you buried.

You don't need to chase rare. You just need to stop leaving it behind.

Let's go.

Coaching Moment: Name What's Already There

This isn't about poetry. It's about truth.

- What's your full name? What story does it carry? Who does it honor?
- What were you called before you believed you earned it?
- Who shaped how you see yourself?
- What identity has been sitting in you, waiting to be claimed?

Final Reflection: Say It Again

You don't need to go searching for your shape in the next chapter.

It's already here.

So slow down. Say your name again—like it means something. Because when you remember who you are:

You move different. You build different. You lead different.

And you stop trying to earn what was already yours.

That's where rare begins.

Chapter 2: Be the Scar, Not the Wound

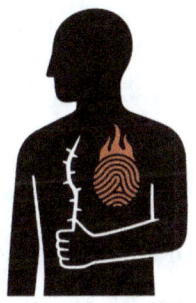

There's pain in the wound. But there's strength in the scar.

Most people want to be rare.

But not many want to talk about the parts that made them that way.

Not the branding moments. Not the curated bio. The hard parts. The disorienting seasons. The decisions that left scars instead of stories.

The moments that still follow you into rooms that have nothing to do with where the pain started.

We've been taught to hide that version of ourselves. To trade it for polish. To tuck away the complicated stuff. To smile and say, "I'm just grateful to be here," even when "grateful" is really code for "I've survived too much to talk about it without breaking."

We've been told those moments disqualify us. That pain makes us fragile. That transparency makes us less hireable, less promotable, less stable.

But that's only true if you're still living in the wound.

The wound is raw. Unfiltered. The wound reacts before it thinks. It's the place where stories get rewritten by shame. Where beliefs about yourself twist into something unrecognizable.

The wound whispers: "You'll never be whole again." "You're too broken to be trusted." "Keep that quiet. They'll think less of you."

But the scar?

The scar tells the truth.

The scar is memory with maturity. It's not just proof that you've been hurt. It's proof that you've healed. That you bled... and didn't stay bleeding.

You lived through what would've broken other people. You cried behind closed doors and still made it to the meeting. You kept praying when God felt silent. You kept building when no one was watching.

And somehow— you made it through.

Not without damage. Not without doubt. But with enough clarity to move forward. Enough strength to stop faking survival and start leading from it.

Let me make this personal.

For years, I believed that to feel legitimate, I had to perform. That if I could just get enough titles—enough external wins—I would finally silence the voice that said I wasn't enough.

I collected achievements like armor. Stacked up certificates. Refined my language. Built my presence.

But when everything was quiet— When I looked at the scoreboard and still felt hollow— That's when I realized something was off.

My most transformational growth didn't come from accomplishments. It came from the silent seasons. The invisible ones. The moments when no one was clapping— and I kept going anyway.

That's where the fire was. Where the rare was formed.

There was a moment I'll never forget.

I had just finished another long meeting where I felt like I was speaking a different language than everyone else in the room. I walked out with fake nods, tight smiles, and a knot in my chest.

And then I sat in my car. Not for five minutes. For almost 45.

No music. No calls. Just silence.

I gripped the wheel without knowing why. My body was still. But everything inside me was pacing. The sun was setting and the light felt wrong—like the day had gotten away from me. Like I had too.

I remember thinking: "What am I even doing here?" "Why am I trying so hard to be digestible when I was never built for small bites?"

It wasn't a breakthrough. It was a break-open.

And I needed it.

Because that's when I stopped asking how to fit. And started asking how to be honest.

That's when I understood something I'd missed my whole life:

My credibility wasn't in my credentials. It was in my scars.

There's a story I've gone back to often when I'm unsure whether survival really counts as strategy.

David and Goliath.

Everyone remembers the slingshot. But we forget the scar.

David wasn't picked because he was fearless. He was picked because he was familiar—with struggle, with survival, with the presence of God.

He wasn't even invited to fight. He was delivering food.

But when he heard the giant, he didn't shrink.

Because David had history. "I've fought a lion. I've fought a bear. And both times, God brought me through."

That's not hype. That's memory turned to muscle.

And when Saul tried to give him royal armor, David didn't just say it didn't fit. He said, "I haven't tested this."

That's discernment. That's spiritual intelligence.

David didn't need someone else's protection. He needed to remember his process.

He reached for what was familiar. For what had already worked in the dark. And he walked toward the giant carrying evidence, not ego.

That's what I want for you.

Not just healing—but honor.

Not just recovery—but readiness.

You didn't go through that for nothing. You didn't come through that season just to "be stronger." You came through it to lead from it.

The scar isn't an afterthought. It's the blueprint.

Coaching Moment: Scar Mapping

Let's break this down.

You're not here to relive pain. You're here to reclaim what it gave you.

And here's a diagnostic to ground you:

If the memory still makes you flinch, it's a wound. If the memory gives you wisdom, it's a scar.

Now ask:

- What have you survived that tried to change the way you see yourself?
- What moments made you question your voice—but also revealed your resilience?
- Where do you still minimize the pain—because it doesn't fit someone else's comfort zone?
- What instincts or strengths were born in the fire?
- If you had to lead with only what you've tested—what's in your hand right now?

This isn't about sounding good. It's about being honest.

Final Reflection: The Scar Is the Strategy

You can't walk in power if you're still pretending nothing happened.

The scar is not your shame. It's your signature.

It says: I've been through the fire. And I'm still here. Not burned up. But burned in.

It says: I've got the receipts. I've got the rhythm. I've got the recovery.

You don't need more polish. You need to stop hiding the proof.

You don't have to wear someone else's armor. You've already been forged.

So lead with what you've tested. Move with what you've survived. And let the scar speak first.

That's rare.

That's you.

Chapter 3: Don't Confuse the Role With the Soul

The role might pay the bills—but your soul carries the weight.

"It feels like we're only getting 40% of you."

That's what my manager said.

And I felt it. Not just in that moment—but in my chest. In every memory of every room I walked into trying to belong, wondering if they could tell I didn't.

Because that line didn't just feel like feedback. It felt like confirmation. Of something I had already been carrying.

That maybe I wasn't enough. That maybe something in me didn't work right.

You can operate at a high level and still feel completely off. You can show up on time, hit your deadlines, get praise— and still feel like you're leaving most of you at the door.

That's what nobody talks about.

They see the outcome, but they don't see the override. The constant gear-shifting. The edits. The masks.

I was a lead data architect. Ran meetings. Delivered results. But I felt like I was functioning in someone else's framework. Like I was showing up for a role—but leaving my soul in the parking lot.

And I thought I was doing what grown folks do.

Show up. Make peace with the stuff that don't feel right. Clock in, clock out. Smile. Perform. Keep it moving.

But there was this static in my chest I couldn't explain. And that 40% comment? It turned the volume up on something I had been trying to mute for years.

Let me be real with you.

Focusing has always been harder for me than it looked. I could lock in. But only sometimes. When I couldn't, I didn't feel distracted—I felt defective.

"Maybe I'm not cut out for this." "Maybe I'm a fraud and it's only a matter of time before everybody sees it."

Especially in rooms full of degrees and polish and people who just looked like they belonged.

Years later, I was diagnosed with adult ADHD. And looking back, I'd been carrying it my whole life without language.

That diagnosis didn't fix everything. But it gave me clarity. And grace.

I wasn't lazy. I was wired different. And different don't mean broken. It means I needed a different design.

So I stopped asking, "How do I become more like them?" And I started asking, "What does success look like for the shape God gave me?"

I started building rhythms. Using tools that helped me stay anchored. Templates. Structure. Boundaries. Quiet.

And when shame came storming back in, I stopped retreating and started asking: "What part of me am I leaving out right now?"

Here's the twist: The very things I thought made me a bad fit... turned out to be my exact strength.

I thought I was just... intense. Turns out, that intensity was precision. I wasn't scattered—I was scanning.

I'm a storyteller—not just to entertain, but to pull truth out of clutter. I'm a coach—because I can see breakthrough coming before the person even sees the need. I'm a problem solver—not because I love puzzles, but because I've had to solve me, more than once.

These aren't soft skills. They're leadership tools. And I didn't learn them in a course. They were formed in fire.

Losing my brother rewired how I understand presence. Not graduating on time? That scarred me. But it also shaped me.

Those wounds became frameworks. That pain became perception.

And when I stopped trimming myself down to fit someone else's mold— I didn't just get louder. I got clearer.

Let me tell you about somebody else.

There was a guy on my team—we'll call him Marcus. Brilliant mind. Quiet, steady energy. But every time he tried to lead like his extroverted peers, he fell flat. He started second-guessing himself. Thought he wasn't "leadership material."

Then one day we sat down. He took the High5 test and got "Thinker" and "Empathizer" at the top.

That's when it clicked.

He didn't need to become more like the loudest voice in the room. He needed to lead like the clearest one.

So we rebuilt his rhythm. He started leading with silence. With reflection. With presence.

And within weeks? His influence tripled. Not because he changed who he was—but because he stopped hiding it.

Now I show up with my strengths and my systems. With clarity and capacity. With real tools that support how I move.

Because being at full capacity? Ain't about being perfect. It's about being whole.

Coaching Moment: Alignment Check

Take a second. Get quiet. Then ask yourself:

- Where am I showing up... but not fully present?
- What parts of me are on mute, and why?
- When's the last time I brought something to the table that didn't fit the job description—but felt fully me?
- Who around me might be adjusting their shape because they think that's what leadership requires?

Now go deeper:

- What do people come to me for—even when I don't offer it as a "skill"?

- Where do I feel the most drained—even when I'm "doing it right"?
- What moments shaped how I show up in tension or transition?
- What would happen if I stopped shrinking to fit the role?

Write it. Voice note it. Whatever you do, don't keep it buried.

Final Reflection: Build What Reflects You

You weren't built to play a part. You were shaped to shift the room.

And your life, your leadership, your legacy—needs the whole you.

Not the edited version. Not the 40%.

When you bring your full shape to the table, everything aligns.

You stop adapting to fit systems that weren't built for you. And you start designing systems that reflect your rare.

That's not rebellion. That's alignment.

And that's how you stop confusing the role... with the soul.

Chapter 4: Your 'Too Much' Might Be Your Edge

Your 'Too Much' Might Be Your Edge.

Your difference might be your differentiator.

Ever walked into a room and edited yourself before you even said hello? Yeah. Me too.

Because somewhere along the way, we got told we were "too much."

Too loud. Too deep. Too intense.

But what if your "too much" is exactly what this moment needs?

Your difference isn't a liability. It might be your leadership. It might be the missing thing the room was waiting for.

And what's wild? Your edge usually shows up everywhere but your job.

You're the coach in your friend group. The one people call when life falls apart. The one who keeps the group chat alive, who asks the question nobody else will. The one who somehow always makes the conversation go deeper.

But come Monday morning? All that gets shelved. You put on your "professional" voice.

You hold your breath to fit someone else's rhythm.

And it's not that you're faking. It's that you've been taught to survive by shrinking.

Let me be real with you.

I used to worry that I was too much. Too opinionated. Too passionate. Too... on.

Even when I wasn't trying to take up space, I was aware that I had presence. And that presence wasn't always welcomed. It made people squirm sometimes. Made supervisors nervous. Made me feel like I needed to turn it down before somebody turned me off.

So I tried. I got quieter. Smaller. More agreeable.

But you know what that got me?

Tired. Disconnected. Misaligned.

Because the truth is—your edge doesn't go away just because you hide it. It just grows sharper in the dark. And if you're not using it to build something on purpose, it might cut you and the people around you by accident.

When I was young, I was called too sensitive. Even my mom worried I'd get eaten up by life because I felt things so deeply. She'd say, "You gotta toughen up, baby." And I tried.

But it turns out, I wasn't broken. I was just empathetic. Highly.

The pain I was feeling wasn't just mine—it was everybody's. I could feel people's energy in a room before they even said a word. I picked up on their judgment, or admiration, or fear, or doubt. Their silence said more to me than their words ever could.

That was a lot to carry as a child. But now? It's a superpower.

As a coach and a leader, that same "too sensitive" trait is what helps me read the room, catch the undercurrent, and meet people exactly where they are.

What they thought was my weakness—was really early evidence of my calling.

Let me tell you what changed it for me.

I started paying attention to what kept showing up. Not on paper—but in patterns.

People didn't just ask me for help on projects. They came for advice. For clarity. For confidence. Not the kind you Google—but the kind you feel when someone just gets it.

They started saying things like, "You always know what to say," or "I feel more clear after talking to you."

And I realized—my edge wasn't a distraction. It was a direction.

You know who lived this out loud? Issa Rae.

Before the world saw her as a mogul, she was uploading "The Misadventures of Awkward Black Girl" on YouTube. It was quirky. Offbeat. Low-budget. Didn't follow any of the "rules."

She didn't look like the Hollywood blueprint. She didn't sound like the TV execs wanted her to.

But she didn't bend to the mold. She built her own.

And what started as "too awkward" became the blueprint for an empire. She made room by being the room.

That's edge.

So now, bring it back to you.

What shows up every time you do—even when you try to leave it outside?

Maybe you explain things in a way that makes people breathe easier. Maybe you shift the vibe without even realizing it. Maybe you hear what people aren't saying—and call it out gently. Maybe you move energy. Maybe you calm it.

That's not random. That's not accidental.

That's not "too much." That's evidence.

Let me bring it even closer.

At one job, I kept getting that same comment: "It's like you bring a different kind of energy to the team."

And it was never said like a compliment. It was said like a caution.

But at the same time, my teammates were pulling me aside—asking for feedback, for help navigating tension, for advice on how to show up more confidently. Not because I was a coach—because I was coaching.

My edge was already leading—long before anyone gave it a label.

And that's when it hit me:

I wasn't "too much." I was just leading from a place they hadn't defined yet.

I wasn't loud. I was clarifying. I wasn't pushy. I was precise. I wasn't intense. I was intentional.

So I stopped trying to fit the list of bullet points in the job description. And I started walking like the edge was the assignment.

The Edge Table: Reframing "Too Much"

What They Called You	What It Actually Is
Too sensitive	Deep emotional intelligence
Too loud	Natural communicator
Too intense	Purpose-driven focus
Too curious	Investigative thinker
Too independent	Self-starter, initiator
Too scattered	Multi-passionate and adaptive
Too serious	Strategic, focused thinker
Too playful	Culture-builder, morale booster

What they couldn't manage might be the very thing that makes you magic.

Coaching Moment: Locate the Edge

Take a breath. Sit with these:

- What do I do so naturally I forget it's even a skill?
- Where have I been told I'm "too much"?
- Where have I hidden something I now know is my gift?
- What do people come to me for—even if it's not my "job"?
- What did I get in trouble for as a kid that turned out to be my gift?

Now try this:

This week, bring one "too much" trait into a space where you usually dim it. Don't wait for permission. Don't water it down. Just bring it. Then watch who responds.

Final Reflection: Stop Shrinking Your Rare

You weren't meant to blend in. You were made to break something open.

What they called "too much" was just early evidence of what you're here to lead.

So talk with your hands. Crack the joke. Start the meeting with a question nobody expects. Be the shift.

Because when you bring your full edge into the room— the room gets sharper.

You're not too much. You're the missing piece they couldn't name—until now.

Phase II: Build Around Your Rare

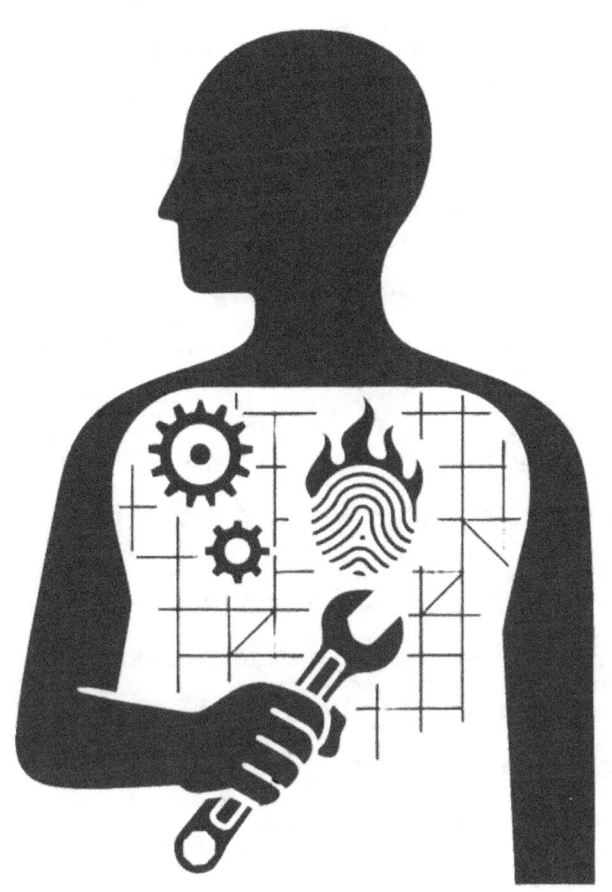

You weren't just made to shine. You were designed to function. To last. To carry weight in real life.

Phase I reminded you of your shape. Now, the real work begins. This isn't about becoming someone new. It's about becoming structured enough to sustain the real you.

You've remembered your rare. Now it's time to build around it. Because rare doesn't thrive in chaos. It needs containers. It needs rhythms. It needs environments where your strengths don't just show up — they lead.

This phase is about shaping your foundation. Designing systems, strategies, and support around who you really are. Not for performance. For sustainability. Not for applause. For alignment.

In the next few chapters, we're getting real about:

– Refining your edge without dulling it – Initiating before you're invited – Building systems that match your wiring – And realizing that your platform might already be right where you're standing

This isn't where you prove your worth. It's where you protect it. Practice it. Pattern it.

Because when you stop editing your shape to fit the system — and start building systems around your shape — you stop bending to fit, and start building what fits you.

You don't just feel aligned. You become undeniable.

Let's build. Not just for now — but for what you're carrying next.

Chapter 5: Refine Your Rare

Turn your "too much" into a tested strength.

Being rare is a gift. But being rare on purpose — That's a calling.

That's the shift. And this chapter? This is where we make it.

You've named your edge. Now we sharpen it. You stop calling it quirky and start calling it strategic. Because when you know the shape of your strength, you stop folding to fit the room— and start forming the room itself.

You ever look back and realize you were flowing, not forcing—and didn't even know it had a name?

That's what discovering your Rare Stack feels like.

It's like finally seeing the blueprint that was always underneath your motion.

The things you thought were random quirks... The instincts that kept showing up even when you weren't trying... The way you do what you do— That's not luck. That's language. That's data. That's design.

And once you name it? You can use it on purpose.

Your Rare Stack is the mix of traits, strengths, and wiring that God designed into you. It's the layered combination of how you think, move, feel, and lead— even when you don't mean to.

It's not a résumé. It's not your personality type. It's the intersection of what comes naturally, what energizes you, and what others trust you with.

Your Rare Stack isn't just who you are. It's how you impact—without pretending. It's how you win—without burnout.

Let me give you the real.

For years, I was moving *in spite of* my Rare Stack. I had instincts, but I didn't trust them. I had strengths, but I downplayed them. I kept trying to trade them for something more "impressive."

You know what that got me? Overthinking. Overcommitting. Underperforming in spaces I was never built to fit. And I started resenting myself for the exhaustion—like it was my fault I couldn't thrive in a system I wasn't shaped for.

But when I started naming my gifts— Not the generic ones, the real ones— Things started locking into place.

My Rare Stack:

- Storyteller – I see the world in scenes, not bullet points.

- Coach – I can hear the part of your story you're skipping.
- Thinker – I need space to reflect before I respond.
- Empathizer – I feel what people carry, even if they never say it.
- Problem Solver – I can see what's broken and I'm wired to fix it, not just observe it.

That's my five. That's my stack.

When I started building my life around that? I stopped chasing roles and started creating lanes.

From "Too Much" to True Strength

I used to believe I was too much. Too talkative. Too deep. Too curious. Too feeling. Too challenging.

But when I started doing this work — really naming how I was wired — I realized something: Those weren't flaws. They were features. They weren't noise. They were signals.

They said you were too talkative — But you were wired to move minds with meaning. You don't just speak — you shift rooms. That's not noise. That's narrative power. *(Storyteller)*

They said you were too deep — But you were built to pull greatness out of people. You don't just see potential — you activate it. That's not heaviness. That's developmental fire. *(Coach)*

They said you were too curious — But you were born to think in frameworks and patterns. You don't just ask questions — you build clarity. That's not distraction. That's discernment. *(Thinker)*

They said you were too feeling — But you were designed to read the room and reach the heart. You don't just feel — you connect and protect. That's not weakness. That's emotional leadership. *(Empathizer)*

They said you were too challenging — But you were wired to go deep, not surface. You don't just confront — you transform. That's not too much. That's root work. *(Problem Solver)*

These aren't accidents. They're assignments.

Your "too much" was never too much. It was the world not knowing what to do with your edge.

Let me tell you about someone I coached.

She was stuck in a director role that looked great on paper but felt heavy. Every Sunday night, her chest would tighten. Not from fear—but from friction. She started questioning if she'd lost her edge—or if she ever had one.

We ran her High5 Test. Her top strengths? Empathizer, Philomath, Coach, Catalyst, Thinker.

She wasn't a bottleneck. She was a builder.™

She didn't need more spreadsheets. She needed more space—to teach, to connect, to spark ideas.

We redesigned her week based on her Rare Stack. She started blocking "thinking hours." Delegated reporting. Scheduled one-on-ones that felt more like strategy jams than status updates.

Her fire came back. And her team? Thrived.

Same role. New rhythm. Stack-aligned.

Here's the point:

Your Rare Stack gives you permission to stop becoming someone else's ideal. And start becoming your designed self—on purpose.

This framework is more than a chapter—it's a compass. One you can return to in every season.

Coaching Moment: Build Your Stack Map

You don't have to guess.

- What do people always come to me for?
- What comes naturally—but feels overlooked?

- Where do I feel most myself?
- Where do I feel friction—even when I'm getting praise?

Then go deeper:

- What are 3–5 words that describe how I naturally lead, think, or connect?
- If I had to name my personal stack right now, what would it be?

Try this:

- Take the High5 Test or revisit your results.
- Create a visual "stack" with your top 5 strengths. Stick it on your wall, desk, or notes app.
- When you're stuck, tired, or triggered—ask: Am I honoring my stack or ignoring it?

Final Reflection: Use It On Purpose

This isn't a flex. It's a formula.

Your Rare Stack isn't something you show off. It's something you show up with.

It's how you hold your lane when the world gets noisy. It's how you stop reacting and start designing.

You've been wired for something specific. And when you move from that wiring?

You don't just operate—you overflow.

Being rare was the gift. Using it on purpose? That's the legacy.

Chapter 6: Don't Wait to Be Picked

***David didn't need a crown to face
Goliath — and neither do you.***

There's a trap high-potential people fall into.
It sounds humble. But it's really just fear in a
flattering filter.

"I just need someone to take a chance on me."
"If they gave me a shot, I'd show up different."
"I'm just waiting for the right opportunity."

That waiting feels noble. But it's really permission-seeking. It's waiting for someone else to validate what you already carry.

And if you sit in that too long... you start shrinking your strengths until they're small enough to be selected. You edit your edge. Mute your brilliance. Hold your breath in rooms where you were built to lead.

That's not humility. That's hesitation dressed up as honor.

Let's call it what it is: You don't need to be picked. You've already been prepared.

The Field Is the Real Training Ground

We all know of the story of David and Goliath. And we also know of the great King David.

Before David ever held a crown, he held a slingshot.

Before the platform, he had the pasture.

He wasn't trained in strategy. Didn't have endorsements. Didn't even get invited to the battlefield.

He was delivering bread. That's it.

But that delivery? It was divine setup.

While his brothers trained for war — David was being trained in the wild. Fighting off bears. Rescuing sheep. Building muscle memory in silence. Learning how to move without applause.

So when Goliath shouted? David didn't flinch.

He wasn't fearless. He was familiar — with his edge, with his Source, with the scars that proved both.

This Is a Goliath Moment

Let's name what's happening around us: It's a Goliath moment.

The pressure's louder. The pace is faster. AI is shifting how we work, how we create, how we lead.

And the whole world is holding its breath, waiting to see what happens next. Degrees don't feel like enough. Titles don't guarantee clarity. Everyone's posting, but very few are moving.

You feel it too, right? That sense that maybe you're not credentialed enough... Maybe you're watching it all unfold and wondering, "Who am I to step in?"

Here's the truth: You've already survived things that should've taken you out. You've already sharpened skills that weren't taught — they were revealed.

This moment isn't asking for the most polished. It's asking for the most prepared. The most aligned. The most obedient to what's already been placed in their hand.

Too many of us are shrinking, second-guessing our gifts, and watching others build things we were designed to lead. And we think the mic will come later—after the promotion, the approval, the permission. But most mics don't come. They're made.

You Don't Need a Crown to Move Like a King

David was anointed long before he was crowned. The oil hit his head in private. Years before the robe ever hit his shoulders.

So when he stepped into the battle — he didn't need Saul's armor.

He knew his shape. He knew what worked. He said: "I can't wear this. I haven't tested it."

He didn't say, "I'm not enough." He said, "This isn't mine."

That's holy discernment. That's real confidence. That's what it means to move like you've already been chosen.

A Story from My Own Field

When I was first hired at Zapier, I had a moment like this. My manager sat me down and said, "Let's look at your strengths. Not your title. Not your tasks. Your shape."

We pulled up my Rare Stack: Storyteller. Coach. Thinker. Empathizer. Problem Solver. And he asked me something nobody had ever asked in a work meeting:

"Where can we make room for these to breathe?"

That question flipped the table. It wasn't about "fitting in" anymore. It was about activating what I already carried.

He told me about the "Big Bets" board — a space for bold ideas. But people weren't speaking up. They were playing small.

That's when I leaned in. I started helping people unlock what they wanted to say. Coached them through clarity. Translated fear into frameworks. Helped them find the right words for their wildest ideas.

It wasn't in the job description. But it was in my design — and that made it undeniable.

I wasn't waiting for someone to tap me. I tapped in.

And the fruit? More alignment. More fulfillment. More fire.

Don't Wait for the Stage. Build the Room

Your strengths don't need approval. They need activation.

You already took the High5 test. You've named your Rare Stack. You know what's in your hand.

So ask yourself: Are you still waiting for the mic? Or are you building spaces where your strengths can speak?

Some of your best work won't happen when you're promoted. It'll happen when you give yourself permission to move before the promotion comes.

You've got the receipts. The wiring. The scars. The stories. You've already been trained in the fire.

Now? It's time to lead like it.

Don't wait to be picked. Walk like you've already been appointed.

Coaching Moment: Move Without Permission

Let's get clear. Where are you still sitting in the back, waiting to be called up?

Write it. Speak it. Sit with it.

- Where in your life are you hoping someone else names what's already obvious in you?
- What have you survived that gave you wisdom the algorithm can't teach?
- What's one room you keep shrinking in — even though you're built to shape it?
- Who's waiting on you to show up full-form, not half-muted?
- What's one bold move you can make this week that honors your Rare Stack?

You're not waiting on permission. You're walking in preparation.

Final Reflection: Faith Moves First

You don't need more armor. You need more clarity.

You don't need a bigger audience. You need alignment.

You don't need to be picked. You need to remember you've already been anointed.

This is your Goliath moment. So don't stall.

Walk into it — not with a crown, but with a sling. Not with applause, but with authority. Not with status, but with scars that say, "I've already been trained for this."

Because once you stop waiting to be picked — you stop shrinking, and start shaping everything around you.

Chapter 7: The System Is You

How I stopped grinding and started designing around my rare

In most work cultures, success sounds like: more discipline. More focus. More structure. More machine. But what if your brilliance doesn't move like that? What if your wiring doesn't match the system? What if your greatest gift—your creativity, your depth, your edge— also comes with dropped threads, mental tabs, or inconsistent rhythm?

That's not dysfunction. That's your design asking for support.

You don't need more shame. You need better structure. Not discipline that punishes. But systems that serve. Not pressure to perform. But design that protects your shape. But design that protects your shape. Because here's the truth: Because here's the truth:You're not just the talent. You're not just the talent.You're the infrastructure. You're the infrastructure.You are the system. You are the system.

From Goals to Systems: A Wake-Up Call

James Clear said it best: "You do not rise to the level of your goals. You fall to the level of your systems."

That hit me like both a rebuke and a release.

Because for years, I had the goals. The ambition. The gifts. But no real system.

I could coach someone through a breakthrough at 2pm... and forget to submit an expense report by 3.

I could write frameworks like fire... but let emails pile up until they became anxiety.

And for the longest time, I thought I was the problem.

Turns out, I was just trying to operate inside systems that weren't built for how I move.

When ADHD Gave Me Language

Getting diagnosed with ADHD as an adult was like turning on a light in a room I didn't know I was sitting in.

Suddenly, everything made sense. I wasn't broken. I was built different. And now I had language for it.

But this wasn't just about ADHD. This was about my entire shape.

Because I wasn't just neurodivergent. I was built with a Rare Stack.

And the job wasn't to manage that— it was to design around it.

Your Rare Stack: Name It Before You Build It

Mine? Storyteller. Coach. Thinker. Empathizer. Problem Solver. That's my rhythm. My blueprint. My real.

What's yours?

Because if you don't design for your shape, you'll default to shame.

Designing Around My Rare Stack

Once I understood my wiring, I stopped asking, "How do I become more focused?" And started asking: "What does my focus need to feel like it belongs here?"

I stopped trying to force brilliance into other people's containers. And started building containers that could catch my brilliance.

Here's how I designed for my Rare Stack:

- Template > Grit: If I do something more than twice, I template it. That's not lazy—that's protecting capacity.

- Energy-Driven Calendar: I block mornings for storytelling and strategy—that's when my Storyteller wakes up.
- Honor the Flow: I time-box coaching sessions and add recovery space after—my Empathizer needs time to breathe.
- Give Strengths a Home: I use voice notes instead of blank docs—my ideas don't always show up in order.

These aren't hacks. They're honor systems. Designed to make room for my real shape.

The Real Point of Systems

Systems aren't just for surviving neurodiversity. They're how strengths stay sustainable.

Self-leadership isn't about powering through. It's about pattern recognition and alignment.

Knowing what drains you. What fuels you.
What triggers your spiral. What unlocks your
spark.

And then building around that data like your
life depends on it. Because sometimes, it does.

Coaching Moment: Build With What You've Been Given

This isn't theory. This is design work. Grab
your notes. Journal. Voice memo. Whatever
works.

Ask yourself:

- Where do I consistently drop the ball, even
  though I care?
- What do I do on my best days without
  forcing it?
- Which parts of my Rare Stack are underfed?

- What have I been trying to "muscle through" that really needs a system or a tool?
- What would be page one of my personal operations manual?

Then ask:

What's one system I could build in the next 48 hours that future-me would thank me for?

Start small. Start real. But start now.

Final Reflection: Build for Your Shape

You don't need to become more like a machine to lead yourself well. You just need to build like someone who believes your shape is sacred.

You're not lazy. You're not scattered. You're not inconsistent. You're not a problem to fix.

You're a system to support. A rhythm to honor. A builder of impact—one boundary, one tool, one shift at a time.

And the more you build around your real, the more your strengths stop feeling like "potential," and start moving like power.

The goal isn't to outwork your wiring. It's to out-design your doubt. I tried batching like a productivity guru. I tried pomodoros. I even tried forcing myself into 5am routines. None of it stuck—because none of it was shaped for me. That's when I stopped asking, "How do I become more focused?" And started asking: "What does my focus need to feel like it belongs here?"

The goal isn't to outwork your wiring. It's to out-design your doubt.

Chapter 8: Your Platform Is Proximity

Big influence starts with being faithful in small rooms.

You don't need to go viral to be valuable.
Sometimes proximity is the platform.
Someone might be catching courage just from
standing close to your authenticity.

Your Presence Already Has Power

A few years ago, I was at a company retreat. It was the meet-and-greet portion—crowded room, drinks in hand, everybody working the circuit with surface-level chatter. The kind of small talk that's expected at these things.

But if you know me, you know—I don't really do small talk. My talk tends to go deep. Fast. And that night was no exception.

I found myself in a corner, locked into conversation with a couple of my direct reports I was meeting in person for the first time. And man... I was just going.

We weren't trading titles or talking weather.

And when it was over, I walked back to my hotel room completely drained. Not because it was bad—but because I thought I blew it.

"Did I overshare? Should I have toned it down? Why didn't I rein it in like you're supposed to at events like this?"

I beat myself up for a while. Thought I made it weird. Thought I did too much.

But a few weeks later, I got a DM on Slack. It was from someone I'd never met before. They said:

"We don't know each other, but I was standing behind you during that conversation at the retreat. You didn't even know I was there. But I just wanted to say—you were saying some of the most interesting things I've ever heard. Being in your proximity that night blessed me. Even though you weren't talking to me, I felt seen."

I didn't realize it at the time—but I wasn't just overheard. I was overheard on purpose.

Proximity Over Platform

That message changed me.

Because I realized: we're so trained to think influence only happens on stages, in viral posts, in front of a mic.

But most of the real breakthroughs? They happen in corners. In whispers. In presence.

And we forget: Proximity is what activates presence. And presence is what multiplies purpose.

You want platform? Start with who's already in the room.

Proximity in Practice

Here are some ways proximity has moved the needle in my own life and leadership:

- Speaking life into a teammate who never asked for coaching—but needed it.
- Holding space for a family member without turning it into a "teachable moment."
- Creating micro-moments of safety on Zoom, even when the camera's off.
- Sending a voice memo that becomes the spark someone carries all week.
- Being present in a group thread—not to prove a point, but to be peace.

You don't need a podium to show up on purpose. You need to be present enough to notice what the room actually needs.

And let's be clear: Your proximity isn't always for the person you're directly addressing. Sometimes it's for the silent listener. The one in the back row. The person scrolling Slack at

2 a.m. catching your courage secondhand. Sometimes it's for the silent listener. The one in the back row. The person scrolling Slack at 2 a.m. catching your courage secondhand.

We Live in a Culture Obsessed with Scale

More followers. More reach. More engagement. More clicks. More likes. More views.

And somewhere in all that noise, we start believing a dangerous lie: "If it didn't go viral, it didn't matter."

But real impact doesn't start with scale. It starts with stewardship. With presence. With who's already listening.

Before you build an audience, build awareness of what your presence already carries.

Before You Reach the Masses, Reach the Middle

I get it. You want your work, your story, your gift to reach far. But God often asks: "Can you be faithful in the middle?"

The middle of a team. The middle of a local community. The middle of a room where nobody reposts you—but they remember you.

Some of my biggest shifts didn't happen because I blew up online. They happened because I showed up in person—present, grounded, listening.

In listening tours, I didn't just hear ideas—I heard fear, vision, frustration. In retros, I didn't just look for what we missed—I looked for who felt missed. In book clubs, I didn't just discuss chapters—I built bridges.

That's not content strategy. That's relational presence. And that's where impact lives.

Fame Can't Replace Faithfulness

There's a reason Jesus didn't start with crowds. He started with twelve. He broke bread before He broke records. He moved town by town before the sermon on the mount.

The algorithm may reward visibility. But the Kingdom honors proximity.

Don't chase influence and miss the invitation to be available. You're not being overlooked. You're being trained to value what won't show up on your analytics.

Because when your character is forged in proximity, you won't need a platform to validate your voice. You'll already know your voice has weight.

Coaching Moment: Where Are You Already Needed?

Let's get honest. Grab your notes.

- Who's already in your life that needs your voice—not your brand?
- Where have you been waiting for "reach" when proximity is already asking for your presence?
- What's one way you can lead, teach, serve, or show up without needing a spotlight?
- What are you stewarding right now that no one sees—but God might be watching closely?
- Where is the impact hiding in plain sight?

Proximity is asking for your attention. Not tomorrow. Now.

Final Reflection: Faithful Where Your Feet Are

Your impact doesn't start when the world knows your name. It starts when the people around you feel your presence.

Your influence isn't measured in impressions. It's felt in who breathes easier when you walk in the room.

So don't let the pressure to be "seen" pull you away from what's already sacred.

Because your greatest platform might be the people who already trust you.

Your Rare Stack wasn't designed just for performance. It was given for proximity. Steward it well. I used to think if it didn't scale, it didn't stick. That it only mattered if it reached thousands. But real leadership isn't about echo. It's about presence.

Phase III — Fully Lit. Fully Led

This isn't when your light begins. It's when your leadership does.

You've remembered your shape. You've built systems to protect and project it. Now it's time to walk in it— publicly, courageously, unapologetically.

This phase is for when traction turns into attention. When your voice carries. When people start looking to you—not just at you.

It's about staying rooted when your Rare becomes visible. About staying whole in systems that want your output but not your essence. About staying human in a world trying to automate the soul out of everything.

Leadership isn't about volume—it's about alignment. It's about alignment. And the courage to keep choosing authenticity over applause, clarity over crowd-pleasing, purpose over performance.

These next chapters will walk with you as you:

- Move forward in tension, even without full clarity
- Navigate visibility without losing identity
- Become the new standard in rooms that weren't designed for you
- Carry your light with integrity—even when the spotlight burns

This is where your shape stops whispering. It starts echoing.

So don't just shine. Shine honest. Shine anchored. Shine like someone who was built for this. Fully lit. Fully led. This isn't the reward. It's the responsibility.

Chapter 9: Let AI Multiply. Let *You* Be the Equation

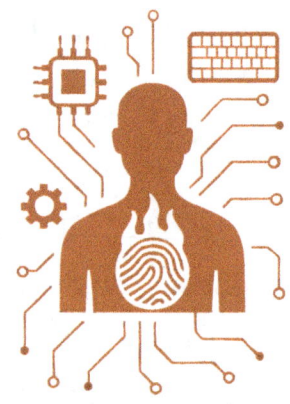

How to hold your humanity when the future's changing fast.

Let's stop dressing panic up as strategy.

Yes — AI is evolving fast. Yes — it will take jobs. Yes — some of the roles you've worked your whole life to grow into might vanish in a wave of automation.

That's not fear. That's reality.

So this chapter? It's not comfort food. It's fuel.

Because you don't need more hype. You need proof that you still matter.

AI isn't just a tech trend. It's a system shift.

And if you're like me, you've felt the pressure: Write faster. Think faster. Code faster. Learn prompts. Stay relevant. Don't fall behind.

Even while writing this book, I had that moment. Not "What if I get replaced?" But: "Am I leaning into something that's going to be uncomfortable?" "Am I building into a future that demands more of me than I'm used to giving?"

That's the real fear. Not losing your job. But stepping into a version of your calling that requires fire — not just skill.

Because here's the truth:

Humans can't be replaced.

You can build a tool that sounds like a coach. You can train a model to mimic a storyteller. But it'll never coach like I do. Never solve like I solve. Never weave memory, metaphor, and lived tension like I can — Because it doesn't have my stories, my scars, my shape. It doesn't know what I've seen. It doesn't carry my cadence. It can't feel what I felt and turn that into clarity for somebody else.

This isn't just a fingerprint. It's a fingerprint on fire.

This isn't just design. It's declaration.

AI can learn roles. But it can't hold rhythm. It can't feel the tension in a room and pivot mid-sentence. It can't call out greatness before someone even sees it in themselves. It can't translate pain into clarity. It can't speak a word in a hallway that saves someone's whole week.

That's human work. That's rare work.

If you wait for the world to validate it, you'll shrink your edge until it's safe again. And safe won't save anybody.

That's why your Rare Stack matters. Not because it feels good to be affirmed. But because when everything's shaking, you need a framework that doesn't fold.

You need to know: What do I bring to every table — even if the table disappears? What kind of value can I create — no matter what the market does? What problems am I built to solve — whether I'm on payroll or not?

Your Rare Stack becomes your strategy.

You don't just say, "I'm a coach." You ask: "How does a coach solve uncertainty right now?"

You don't just say, "I'm a storyteller." You ask: "Who needs a narrative that helps them remember who they are?"

Rare doesn't mean soft. It means specialized. It means when everyone else panics — you pivot with purpose.

Let's challenge a myth: "The smarter AI gets, the less humans are needed." False.

The more powerful AI becomes, the more it needs human touch. It needs your discernment. Your judgment. Your emotional intelligence. Your Rare Stack.

There are three primary ways AI shows up in work today:

• Automation — Rule-based systems that follow predefined steps with no decision-making. Great for repetitive, structured tasks. • AI Workflows — Tools that use machine learning or natural language processing within set boundaries. Still require human prompts, guidance, and review. • AI Agents — Refers to LLM-driven or multi-model systems that can plan, take actions, make decisions, and react dynamically. Still require oversight, alignment, and grounding in human judgment.

So no — you don't disappear in the next version of the world. You become even more essential to how it functions.

Coaching Moment: Design Your Response, Not Just Your Résumé

You're not playing defense. You're building response systems.

Ask yourself:

• If AI replaced your role, what would still be true about you? • What part of your Rare Stack do people come to you for — without asking? • Who's in uncertainty right now that your shape was made to support? • What feels risky... but also feels like you? • What's one move you can make this week to put your Rare in the wild — publicly, practically, unapologetically?

It could be a post. A conversation. A prototype. A pitch. A message that says, "Hey, I've been thinking about how I can help."

Let AI multiply. But let you be what's worth multiplying.

Final Reflection: Don't Be Afraid to Build Anyway

You're not fragile. Your calling isn't either.

You've made it through:

• layoffs • pivots • reorgs • burnout • systems that didn't fit • cultures that couldn't hold your shape

You didn't survive all that just to freeze because machines got smarter.

AI is fast — but it's not free. It costs connection. Creativity. Conviction.

You may take your time — but you carry depth. You carry discernment. You carry divine assignment.

So no — you don't have to compete with the machine. But you do have to show up.

Because someone is looking for you right now. Not the polished version. Not the AI-trained version. The present one. The practiced one. The rare one.

Let the tools grow. Let the systems scale. But don't shrink. Because the most powerful system is still a rare one — living on purpose. For me, it was the reorg in 2020. My role shifted overnight, and all the structure I had built my value around disappeared. But what stayed? People still came to me for clarity. For coaching. For the way I see systems and synthesize chaos into clarity. That's when I knew—I wasn't just good at my job. I was carrying something that didn't vanish when the job did.

Chapter 10: No Map. Still Moving.

Thriving through uncertainty, alignment, and intentional movement.

Most of us are trying to follow purpose like there's a map. But what we're really carrying... is a compass.

Clarity is a privilege. Alignment is a decision. And sometimes, walking in purpose feels like walking through fog — with nothing but a whisper of direction in your chest.

We want the plan. We want the proof. We want the spreadsheet to go with the sermon. We want structure and spiritual at the same time.

But what if the vision's clear — and the path isn't?

What do you do when your Rare starts pulling you in a direction your industry doesn't recognize, your mentors don't understand, and your résumé can't fully explain?

That's where I lived. For years.

Wrestling With the Shape

I wrestled. And I don't say that lightly. I mean wrestled.

Do I stay rooted as a data engineering leader — where the titles are clear, the roles are defined, and the pay is stable?

Or do I lean fully into coaching — what I know I am, but what feels unproven, unsafe, and honestly... not a role most tech companies are actively hiring for?

Or do I find a third way — a shape that holds both? A role that's not on a job board. Not in the promotion pipeline. Not pre-approved by HR. But fully, unmistakably me.

I chose the third way: the aligned shape.

And it was risky.

I'm still learning as a manager. Still building technical depth. But I'm also leading with my Coach, Storyteller, Empathizer core.

Not because someone handed me the perfect title... but because I stopped waiting for a map and started trusting my rhythm.

You Don't Need a Map. You Need a Compass.

Maps tell you: "Here's the route. Follow these steps. Get here safely." Compasses tell you: "This is true north. Start moving."

And that's what I had to do.

Every time I leaned into coaching — writing this book, mentoring my team, speaking what needed to be said — I felt aligned.

Even when it didn't look promotable. Even when it didn't look profitable.

I didn't have the staircase. But I had the next step.

That's what Rare does.

It doesn't always give you a blueprint. It gives you direction.

And fear doesn't leave the equation. It walks with you.

We talk about David and Goliath like it was a clean kill. But what if David missed? What if that stone just grazed Goliath's shoulder? What if David had to scramble — heart pounding — to reload the sling before the giant closed the distance?

It could've happened.

But he stepped up anyway. Not because it was guaranteed. But because he had history with God. He had rhythm with who he was.

Courage doesn't cancel fear. It just moves anyway.

Alignment Over Answers

We all want certainty. But certainty is a myth.

What's real? Alignment.

Moving in a way that matches your shape even when it doesn't match your surroundings.

You might not see step ten. But if step one feels like peace, if step two sounds like obedience, if step three lights up your Rare Stack — you're on the right path.

Sometimes clarity isn't what you carry. It's what shows up after the third or fourth bold move.

Sometimes the light doesn't turn on until your foot hits the floor.

Coaching Moment: Move Anyway

This one's for the fog-walkers. The pivot-dwellers. The blueprint builders who don't have the blueprint yet.

What part of you is ready to move, even if the path isn't mapped?

- Name the tug. What's the compass?
- What direction points to more alignment with your Rare Stack?
- What "orthodox shapes" have you been shrinking into? What's not working anymore?

- Where could you show up more fully this week — even if no one's asking you to?
- What's one next faithful move — not the whole plan, just the next step?

Don't wait for confirmation to move. Move and let confirmation meet you on the way.

Final Reflection: Walk It Out Anyway

You might not have the title. The timeline. The clarity. The confidence.

But you've got something better:Alignment.Conviction.Rhythm.Faith.

And that's enough to move.

You don't need every stair to show. Just the faith to take one. You just need the step.

So take it.

The map may come later. But the compass is already in your chest.

Point toward your shape. Move like you believe it.

Even if the lights don't turn on right away — trust that the path will catch up to your steps.

This is how Rare walks. By compass, not consensus. If peace keeps surfacing when you think about it, that's worth more than 100 endorsements.

Chapter 11: Be the Benchmark

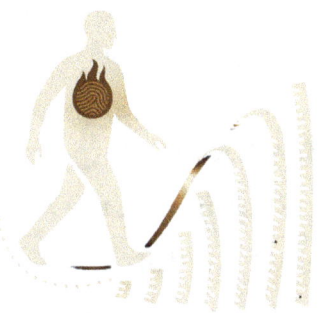

Don't measure up. Redefine the standard.

There comes a point in your rare journey where you stop asking, "Do I measure up?" And you start declaring: "This is the measure now."

Because somewhere along the way, we were taught to measure everything:

• How fast you move • How loud you are • How many people follow you • How "professional" you sound • How well you fit

So we walk into rooms and roles constantly asking: "Am I doing this right?" "Do I sound like I belong here?" "Do I look like what they're used to seeing?"

But here's what I've learned: When you're Rare, blending in isn't the assignment. Standing out—and standing up—is. You're built to stand out—and stand up as the new example.

You don't just meet the standard. You move the standard.

From Mirror to Model

You've spent this whole book looking inward: Clarifying your Rare Stack. Building systems around your shape. Walking without a map. Moving with no blueprint. Saying yes when it still felt risky.

Now comes the flip.

It's no longer just about how you see yourself.
It's about how others start to see what's
possible—because of you.

You become a mirror for others to recognize
their shape. You become a model of what Rare
leadership looks like in real motion.

Not loud. Not flashy. Just rooted. Real.
Repeating the rhythm of your alignment.

I'll never forget the moment someone said to
me, "I didn't know I could lead this way until I
saw you doing it."

That's when I knew—this wasn't just about me
finding my shape. It was about giving other
people permission to move in theirs.

Who Told You That Was the Standard?

Let's interrogate this:

• Who told you your voice was "too much"? • Who told you coaching wasn't technical enough? • Who told you leadership looks like charisma + control? • Who told you your story didn't count unless it came with a title?

Because most "standards" are just recycled preferences. And a lot of them were built without people like you in mind.

So no—you don't need to measure up. You need to redefine up.

You're not here to match their model. You're here to offer a new one.

When you walk in your Rare, you remind the room: "We don't all lead the same. We don't all speak the same. We don't all move the same. And that's the point."

You've Been Dodging the Light

Here's another layer: Most people don't struggle to be powerful. They struggle to accept that they already are.

You know how I know? Because we've been trained to diminish the light.

Someone compliments us—and we shrink. "You're amazing at that," becomes "Ah, it's nothing." "You helped me so much," becomes "I'm just doing my part."

So let me ask you something I always ask my coaching clients: What if you went back through your life and fully received every compliment you've ever been given?

Not the polite version. Not the half-nod. All of it.

That teacher who said you were a leader That boss who said your presence shifted the room That friend who said you helped them survive the week

What if all of it landed? Where would that light have projected you? Where would it have propelled you?

What would you believe about yourself? What would you have built?

Now flip it forward: If you start fully receiving the truth of who you are today... If you stop dodging the light and let it hit you full force... Where could your life go from here?

And while you're at it: Start giving the compliments you used to withhold too. Because when you're the benchmark, you don't just shine. You ignite. You multiply light by giving it away.

The Cost of Leading Like You

Let me tell you right now—being the benchmark isn't easy.

People will misunderstand you before they model you. You'll be overlooked because no one's seen it done your way. You'll be questioned because your rhythm won't match theirs. You'll be tempted to shrink, just to get seen faster.

But if you keep showing up in your shape, with consistency, clarity, and conviction...

Eventually, people stop trying to fit you into their mold. And they start asking for your blueprint.

Coaching Moment: Be It Anyway

This isn't about ego. It's about embodiment.

- Where have you been waiting for someone else to validate your leadership before you believed it?
- What standard are you tired of trying to meet—and ready to rewrite?
- Who around you might be watching your Rare... hoping it gives them permission to move in theirs?
- Where are you already the example—whether you own it or not?
- What would change if you walked like your way was the way?

Remember: the moment you own it is the moment they believe they can too.

Final Reflection: You Are the Example

You don't have to imitate influence. You are influence.

You don't have to keep auditioning for a standard that was never built for you. You're here to build a new one.

Be the example of leadership that's emotionally intelligent, not just strategic. Be the leader who creates clarity—without needing the spotlight. Be the example of what Rare looks like in real motion.

You're already shaped for this. You're already positioned to lead.

Now show them how Rare walks—by compass, not consensus. Light multiplies through reflection. Don't hoard it. Pass it forward.

Chapter 12: Fully Lit, Fully Led

How to stay grounded when your rare gifts start to shine.

Let's pause here. Before we go into the light, let's anchor ourselves in what got us here.

The scariest part of success isn't being seen. It's staying yourself once the light hits.

There's a kind of fear nobody talks about. It doesn't show up when you're failing. It shows up when you start winning.

When the door opens. When the platform grows. When the inbox floods. When people start quoting your words like scripture. When they treat your voice like a compass.

That's when it hits: "Am I built for this? Can I hold this light without losing myself in it?"

Welcome to the paradox: You prayed for this. You paid for this. Now you have to protect this.

The Light Can Blind You

Visibility doesn't just magnify your voice. It magnifies your vulnerabilities too.

When Identity Becomes a Product

In the AI era—where efficiency is king and identity is often reduced to brand—you will be tempted to become a product instead of a person.

That's the pressure:

• To stay viral • To stay relevant • To stay useful • To stay enough

But hear me: You weren't built to be useful. You were built to be whole.

Your Rare wasn't given for performance. It was given for purpose. And purpose must be stewarded, not streamed.

So don't just be lit. Be led.

Led by conviction. Led by rhythm. Led by something eternal—not algorithmic.

Don't Get Famous for a Fabrication

You can get known for what's profitable and lose what's prophetic. You can build reach and lose resonance. You can get paid for being polished while the real you starts starving.

So here's the warning: Don't get famous for a version of you that doesn't even feel alive.

That's not Rare. That's replication.

Rare doesn't hide from the light. But it doesn't fake it either.

It reflects the light. It filters it. And it returns it with grace.

Rare Isn't a Brand. It's a Burden—and a Blessing.

If you build your platform but forget your personhood, you will reach many... and still feel alone.

The Cost of Being Rare Is Real

Let's talk about it.

Being Rare can feel lonely. Leaning into your shape can feel isolating.

There's a very human pull to want to blend in. To feel safe. To be understood.

Because standing out comes at a cost.

But you're not the only one paying it. You're not the only one walking different. You're just one of the few who's doing it on purpose.

Now ask yourself:

What's the reward of fitting in... versus the reward of being Rare?

Fitting in might earn you comfort. Predictability. A clean résumé.

But being Rare? Being you on purpose?

That creates impact. That builds legacy. That gives others permission to breathe.

And that's worth the discomfort.

Because the alternative is too expensive: A life where you were seen, but never known.

The Call Is Heavy. Build for It.

The higher your platform rises, the deeper your roots must go.

That means:

• Boundaries • Sabbath • Stillness • People in your life who don't care about your metrics

You can't outsource obedience. You can't automate discernment. You can't GPT your soul work—because discernment doesn't scale. It roots.

And if you've made it this far, you already know: Rare isn't a brand. It's a rhythm. It's a resistance. It's a way of being in a world that would rather flatten you than free you.

So don't just shine bright. Shine honest. Shine anchored.

Coaching Moment: Stay Whole at Full Wattage

- Where are you most tempted to overperform now that people are watching?

- What rhythms help you remember you're a person, not a platform?
- Who has permission to call you back to your core when you start drifting?
- What values must remain non-negotiable as you grow?
- What does "being led" look like practically in your next season?

Final Reflection: The World Needs What You Carry

You are not a machine. You are not a moment. You are a movement. A living, breathing, story-shaped force.

And now you are fully lit. People see it. So shine. Move rooms. Carry weight.

But don't lose your rhythm. Don't carry what was never yours.

Lead like your shape was sent. Love like your light heals. Speak like your voice still echoes when the algorithm forgets you.

And when the spotlight hits? Don't flinch. Don't shrink. Don't disappear.

You've been prepared for this. You're rare on purpose.

This isn't the end of your Rare. It's the beginning of how it shows up for others.

Now go be fully led. So lead like you're not surprised to be here.

Go Be Rare

You've looked in the mirror. You've named what's always been there. You've stopped shrinking and started sharpening. You've learned to move without maps, to lead without masks. To shine without performing. To carry without overcompensating.

And now comes the part only you can do: Go build what didn't exist until you showed up. Go coach. Write. Lead. Create. Restore. Disrupt. Be the blueprint they didn't know they needed.

Even when it costs you clarity. Even when they misunderstand you. Even when it would be easier to go back to the box.

You've been called to this. And you've been crafted for this.

In an age of automation, distraction, and imitation— Showing up fully in your Rare is a revolutionary act.

You didn't just read a book. You remembered your shape.

To the Coaches. The Empathizers. The Builders. The Quiet Anchors. To the Wild Dreamers. The Finishers. The Timekeepers. There's a reason you've been shaped like this. Not for attention. Not for applause. But for impact.

You don't need more permission. You've got alignment. You don't need more polish. You've got purpose.

So stay rooted. Stay rare. Stay ready.

And when the world asks for more of the same? You answer with something they never planned for: your unedited, unmistakable Rare.

Rare doesn't end here. It lives in how you walk from this page.

Now go be Rare—on purpose. And now you're accountable for what you carry.